the

Vision

Outlining & organizing
your ministry

Wayne C. Anderson

Copyright © 2018 Wayne C. Anderson

Published by Standsure Press
3313 W Cherry LN #656
Meridian ID 83642
USA
standsureministries@standsure.net

All rights reserved.

ISBN: 1724470027
ISBN-13: 978-1724470027

Scripture quotations translations of the author and the Authorized Version or King James Version

Scripture quotations taken from the New American Standard Bible®, Copyright © 1960, 1962, 1963, 1968, 1971, 1972, 1973, 1975, 1977, 1995 by The Lockman Foundation. Used by permission." (www.Lockman.org)

NKJV Scripture taken from the New King James Version®. Copyright © 1982 by Thomas Nelson. Used by permission. All rights reserved.

This book's cover was lovingly prepared by

Anita Lee Johnson

Please visit learning.iamtheway.org
For the online course by this title

CONTENTS

Table of Contents

PREFACE	I
1 WRITE THE VISION	1
2 DEFINING YOUR CORE VALUES	16
3 DEFINING YOUR PURPOSE	21
4 DEFINING YOUR VISION	29
5 DEFINING YOUR MISSION	38
6 LET'S WRITE THE CHARGE	46
7 CONSULTING APOSTLES & PROPHETS	60

To the shepherds who serve the Great Shepherd of the Father's own flocks.

Please do not weary in well doing.

Preface

This book is meant to be a kind of workbook for the leader to start the process of founding a church, a ministry or even a business in partnership with the Holy Spirit. It is the result of decades of experience and study on the subject.

Something I've taught most of my life is that if you fail to plan you plan to fail. I build business plans for almost everything I do. That planning causes me to have success or stops me before I get into trouble.

This book goes with an online course by the same title found on our website at:

learning.iamtheway.org[1]

I would strongly suggest that you also signup for this online course since there

---

[1] Available to the public for a fee but free to members of our network, International Apostolic Ministries.

will be much more interaction and continued education available there.

When Yehovah told Habakkuk the prophet to "write the vision," and to "inscribe it on tablets," He didn't say it would be easy to do so. After all, Yehovah added that the purpose of writing the vision was so that someone could read it an run with it. None of this process was easy for Habakkuk. It's not going to be easy for you either.

True, you are inspired by the Holy One to formulate your ministry according to the vision that He has communicated with you. But like Habakkuk, you now need to write and inscribe on tablets and work it out so that it makes others run with it. This "writing" is going to be an investment on your part.

I have specifically tried to make this book short and not so wordy so as not to be more labor for you. I think that each paragraph is essential but may need more dialogue. For this reason, I've constructed the online course.

Please enjoy the process in which you find yourself. You can do this, and you can do it well. Even while I'm typing this, my Grammarly encourages me that "To err is human; to edit is divine." Ha.

Also, please remember that once you think you are done and can now get to work and ministering you will find that you need to go back and add to-subtract from much of what you initially write. I have come to enjoy how ministry is organic and grows with time and life itself.

My sincere hope is that this helps you to build your ministry and have more success in your eyes than what you expect.

Don't worry. Be happy.

1 Write the Vision

"I will stand upon my watch, and set myself upon the tower, and will watch to see what He will say unto me, and what I shall answer when I am reproved. And the LORD answered me, and said, 'Write the vision, and make it plain upon tablets, that he may run that reads it. For the vision is yet for an appointed time, but at the end, it shall speak, and not lie; though it tarries, wait for it; because it will surely come, it will not delay.'"
Habakkuk 2:1 – 3

"Write the things which you have seen, and the things which are, and the things which shall be hereafter;"

Revelation 1:19

"For whatsoever things were written aforetime, were written for our learning, that we through patience and comfort of the scriptures might have hope. Now the God of patience and consolation grant you to be likeminded one toward another according to Christ Jesus: That you may with one mind and one mouth glorify God, even the Father of our Lord Jesus Christ."

Romans 15:4 - 6

"Now I plead with you, brethren, by the name of our Lord Jesus Christ, that you all speak the same thing, and that there be no divisions among you, but that you be perfectly joined together in the same mind and in the same judgment."

1 Corinthians 1:10 (NKJV)

Writing the vision will cause your ministry to grow.

Although there are over thousands of words in this book to help you write your ministry vision, it is written for the express purpose of explanation and to simplifying the process of skillfully planning the success of your ministry.

This is not an easy job but, believe me; it is easier to do this now than vacilate and roam through the day-by-day struggles of life and ministry without a plan. More effort and energy will be spent if you do not successfully write out a clear and concise ministry plan than if you do. To do it now will be of great relief to you and those around you.

For the best results, I strongly suggest you:

- ✓ Read this entire book through.
- ✓ Collect any tools that you will need to accomplish the work described.

- ✓ Use a legal pad/paper tablet if possible for notes and design.
- ✓ Go away to a place of solitude, without disturbance; to write answers to the questions.
- ✓ Complete the questions with appropriate answers. (This is not a test. This is for your benefit.)
- ✓ Build and publish your own Vision.

Note: Answer the questions on your notepad. You'll probably want to re-write your articulations several times. Don't be super-spiritual in your answers. Make your statements plain, simple, descriptive and capable of being understood. Try to use common social language instead of churchy talk.

About What We Are Doing Here

What you have here is a kind of workbook that can be used for establishing a new ministry work orchestrated by God the Father through you. Many have used it for reorganizing an existent ministry as well. It is for the foundations of a church plant, an existing church, an independent home group, church or an "out of the church experience." Ha! Some still use the term, "para-church ministry," but I think there are better descriptions for those many types of ministries that work alongside churches in a region but are not an actual church body.

'This is also an excellent reference for itinerate ministers, and even the establishment of a business that is formed for the sake of the Kingdom of God.

For all of this I'd like to use the term; "church/ministry" to accommodate the many purposes.

Inscribe it! Write it!

As Habakkuk says, "write the vision!" It is best that you use this document as a workbook for the laying of a foundation to build the ministry of effectiveness that you have desired. Your goal here is to write these things out concisely. Once we have accomplished this, we can build.

The establishing of your ministry/church is the first of some very vital work that is to be done. Laying the foundation is not the most fun part of a building, but it is the most crucial part. The depth, the size, the strength of that foundation, determines what will be built upon it for the world to see.

It is important that we settle some basic, yet essential, issues before we lay the first stones of this foundation. If we set some basic standards and beliefs, we will not waver from the vision and purpose of the ministry that God has given.

Now, at first, you may not know where the answers to these questions might come. However, through prayer and consideration, as well as discussing them among you at some creative moments, we are sure that the answers will flow. These answers will come from heaven, from the heart, and a little bit from the head (but only a little).

There is no way around this foundation-laying work. The sooner it gets done, the sooner your ministry can be adequately constructed. So, roll up your sleeves, and let's get going!

The question here is: "What is the Holy Spirit saying?"

The most important part of building this foundation and writing the vision down is the documentation of the word of the Holy Spirit that is coming to you. The voice of His Spirit may range from a simple statement, which you can explain in detail, to the description of a visitation, which could take pages to assimilate.

Dreams, visions, or trances are a part of the language of the Holy Spirit and should be described and commented on if they are pertinent to the workings of the ministry. Any prophetic utterances should be collected and written down, along with the "super desires," since God gives us the desires of our hearts.

A word to the wise is "don't over-think these things!" Let your heart flow with what the Holy Spirit is want to focus on in the "now" moment.

Let's get to work. First of all, let's recall what the Holy Spirit has said.

- What has the Holy Spirit said through Prophecy?
- What has the Holy Spirit said through the voice of God to your heart?
- What has the Holy Spirit said through visions and dreams?
- What is in your heart?
- What are your desires?
- What do other people say your skills are?
- What do you say of each other's skills?
- What is your inheritance?

Once you have spent a considerable amount of time giving answers to all or most of these questions and you have written notes on your notepad, we can begin to establish the following issues:

- Core Values
- Purpose
- Vision
- Mission

These issues are the standards of your heart. They become "the Why, the What & the How,"[2] that is so important to others. After all, the ministry isn't really about you, is it? No, it is about others, it is for others, and it is accomplished with others.

You may want to research some examples from other similar ministries to help you arrive at your own. It is not a sin to use another's words to inspire you, but they must become your own in truth and in spirit (and you should be mindful of copyright infringements and not set out to be plagiaristic).

---

[2] Simon Sinek: startwithwhy.com

Consult the pages that follow for the definitions of these key terms and a kind of creative atmosphere in which to work. We will work to answer the following questions:

A. What are your core values?

B. What is your purpose in ministry?

C. What is your vision?

D. What is your mission?

Let's start with the WHY

There is a dynamic teacher that is influencing the business world today by the name of Simon Sinek. I strongly suggest you listen to his TED Talk and find his teaching on YouTube as well as read his book "Start with WHY."[3]

---

[3] Start with WHY: How Great Leaders Inspire Everyone To Take Action, By Simon Sinek. Published by the Penguin Group Penguin Group (USA) Inc., 375 Hudson

Simon articulates what I've tried to present in this book in a unique and inspiring way. He says what I've always believed. If you don't know Why you do what you do, then it really doesn't matter much in how well you do it or the way that you do it. Yet, I know very few people in ministry that can articulate the why of their lives and ministry. Those who can openly describe the why of their ministry will always have partners and loyal followers, as well as great success in accomplishing the tasks that their ministry is designed to do.

Simon's WHY is actually an acronym for:

W - What you do

H - How you do it

Street, New York, New York 10014, U.S.A.. Available on Amazon.com and bookstores everywhere.

Y - Why you do what you do

The most important of these and that which should be first on your list to decide, design and articulate is your "Y-Why." Your What and your How should come from that Why.

https://startwithwhy.com

In the first two questions that I propose to you are to help you know and understand your Why.

A. What are your core values?

B. What is your purpose in ministry?

Your "core values" will help you establish the foundation of understanding why you are founding this ministry. From your "core values" should come your "purpose" and you will be able to state why your ministry exists. You can then tell others, and they will be quite apt to partner with you because they believe in why you do what you do.

The next two questions will help you to outline your plan to succeed in ministering from your why. In other words, your why is the driving force to send you out into the world to accomplish the will of God on earth as it is in heaven, but you'll need to design what to do and how to do it. So, the questions:

What is your vision? - Should help you define what you do.

What is your mission? - Should help you define how you do what you do.

But, everyone in ministry does stuff, and some do it better than others. Believe it or not, the majority of people don't much care about how well they do it or even what it is they do. People care about why you do what you do in ministry.

So, now let's get started on defining your core values.

2 Defining Your Core Values

Your "core values" are those genuine issues, which are your convictions. The principles, which you are prepared to die for, in seeing them given out to the world.

These "core values" are those few things that you just don't compromise and have become the issues that drive you to do a work for God. Realize that these "core values" are not the kind of fundamental Christ beliefs that are your soul saving convictions.

What I mean is, you don't need to list your faith in the Blood of Jesus, your belief that He is the only one true God, etc. Later you'll develop your statement of beliefs which will take care of this side of things.

Instead, these "core values" are the convictions that you have which cause you to want to establish your ministry/church and gather others to have your same convictions. These are truths that you will always hold near and dear. These are your life messages. They can even be the things you feel need to be said or done and are most important to the world around you.

Please understand that one should never establish their "core values" based on their correction or comparison to others. How fragile our lives and ministries would be if we spent our lives correcting the course of other ministries instead of correcting the path of sinners that are heading for disaster!

In short, there are some to whom holiness is their most valuable issue in life. To some, it would be depths of prayer or hearing the voice of God. Yet others would say, sacrificial giving to the poor; and so on.

A few years ago, two of my closest friends asked me to list my three most prominent life messages after 40 years of ministry. It didn't take me long to give them an answer. I said, "The Substance of Heaven, The Table of the Lord and Prayer & Intercession." Both friends wholeheartedly agreed, and they told me to concentrate my efforts to produce these messages unto the nations in every way possible.

These are the "Core Values" of my life and ministry. Although I do a lot of things, I'm known more for my "Core

Values" than any or all of the other things that I do and may show some measure of expertise.

These "core values" borderline with your purposes except that your purpose will target your actions. We should not separate our Purpose from our Core Values. Instead, we should help give definition and explanation.

You might search for some examples of these "core values" from other ministries and businesses to get some clear ideas about your own.

Irene and I have an established personal ministry by which we do most of the works of our ministry. It is called Standsure Ministries. From what I shared with you above about the three life messages, you will find them to be our core values:

Standsure Ministries with Wayne C. & Irene Joy Anderson

Our Core Values are:

> - The substance of the Father's love
> - The Table of the Lord
> - Prayer & Ecclesia Intercession

So, what are your core values? Perhaps you can write down ten different core values and prioritize them and then choose the top 3-5. Go ahead. Give it a try. When you are done, we'll build upon them with our purposes next.

3 Defining Your Purpose

Your Purpose is your reason for being in the ministry. Why are you going to do it? These purposes may be several in number but don't try to cover everything that you think you might try to do in the future. That is Vision stuff - the what you do and how you do it is coming later.

Every church/ministry/business should have a plan to affect the earth in some way. The confidence of leadership is constructed upon this knowledge of the consequence of this ministry/business to our world around us.

The question of "Why another church/ministry?" is sure to come to you from both the outside and from the inside of your organization or from those with whom you minister. The question needs to be settled in your mind and heart as well as in the minds and hearts of those who will work in partnership with you. It is essential that you know what the need is that can be met by the vision, which the Holy Spirit has given you.

Please be careful not to spend any time comparing what you will do with the church/ministry next door. There is no room for spiritual supremacy in the Kingdom of heaven, and it is a snare of the trapper that will end in defeat and failure. There is no room in the kingdom of God for a competitive spirit, so don't compete.

You really need to take an honest look at

what you can do to enhance and advance the Kingdom of God in your city and region. There is more work to do than what is being done, so, there is always room for another church, another service, another ministry a new business.

No church/ministry should ever be built upon a person's need to preach or minister. If the voice inside you is saying, "I need to do this," you have the wrong approach. The Father of lights gives perfect gifts to His children. You and your ministry should be seen as one of those perfect gifts.

The only reason that our heavenly Father would want you to build a church/ministry is that those whom He loves are in need of it. As an example, Abba doesn't certify a church plant in a neighborhood so that one of His children has a place to preach and express themselves in ministry. He loves the people of that neighborhood and wants one of His children to be His voice to those whom He loves.

So, take another look at your "core values" and start making notes on what needs should be met from them. We build our ministry purposes from our core values. That's how it works. Then we can articulate why we exist as a ministry and why we do what we do.

As an ongoing example, this is how the core values and the purposes of ministry go together for Standsure Ministries. As you can see in this example, they are not carbon copies of each other. They are like collecting the crucial bits of information that culminate into a whole beautiful picture.

Standsure Ministries with Wayne C. & Irene Joy Anderson,

Our Core Values are:

> ➢ The substance of the Father's love

- The Table of the Lord
- Prayer & Ecclesia Intercession

The Purpose of this ministry is:

- To be a father and encourage others to become fathers of the faith to many
- Restore Kingdom Family values to the earth
- Reveal and instruct toward effective Ecclesia courts of heaven intercession
- The abiding presence of Jesus for Revival
- Reveal and teach the miracle healing presence of Jesus & bring revival to people groups, churches, cities & nations

I have developed our ministry purposes from our core values. You should be able to see each of our core values in each of our ministry purposes to varying degrees. So that you know, my heart feels each of my core values in every statement of purpose. After writing the purpose statements, I read them to make sure I feel my core values in each one. Then I read them backward to be sure.

Now, we can articulate the "Why." We will develop the "Why" statement from our Core Values and Purpose of ministry.

Standsure Ministries with Wayne C. & Irene Joy Anderson

Why does our ministry passionately exist?

- ➢ We believe for a movement to take place and that the substance of the love of the Father is manifestly displayed upon the earth through calculated acts of love toward others.

- We believe that the Passover/Communion that Jesus Christ fulfills in us as believers will have the same delivering effects as when the children of Israel were delivered from their bondage in Egypt. Even so, people's lives are changed in this great movement when believers partake of the bread and the cup of Christ which announces the believer's deliverance and liberty.

- The Ecclesia of Christ is emerging in this hour. There are measurable effects of prayer and intercession at the level of the courts of heaven which are being manifest upon the earth, and we can change the world with prayer.

- The destruction of the family must be reversed and we have many teachers but not many fathers.

Therefore we are raising up fathers in partnership with the Holy Spirit to repair the torn down families and give comfort, strength and revive each aspect of the family by the authority of the Father's Kingdom.

- We are convinced that our dedication to manifest the love of the Father in these ways will bring a revival of the Father's love to churches, people groups, cities & nations.

With some research, you should be able to find online other examples that are even better or more applicable to your needs. The time you spend on designing your core values, your purposes and then articulating your why is tremendously valuable and will give growth to your prosperity.

Now it is time to move on so that we can define your vision.

4 Defining Your Vision

*"And the Lord answered me, and said,
'Write the vision,
and make it plain upon tablets,
that the one who reads it may run.'"*

Habakkuk 2:2

Vision. I like to call this the God stuff. From your intimate times with the Holy Spirit, He partners with you to see what is happening in the future as a result of accomplishing your purpose for ministry? In other words, you can see your why working and accomplishing the works of the Kingdom of heaven upon the earth.

Prophet Habakkuk or Isaiah saw extreme and heavenly things pertaining to the future of humanity. That which you see may not be so extreme, but it is nonetheless critical to humanity - those who will be affected by your ministry.

John Wimber was a professional musician who suddenly fell in love with Jesus Christ. He consumed the New Testament and wanted to know where he could join up with people to "do the stuff" - that is "the stuff that Jesus did." What he meant by the stuff was the miracles of healing and the manifestation of the love of the Father upon the earth. John searched but couldn't find people with whom he could do the Jesus stuff. So, Wimber just began to do the stuff himself, and he was responsible for a move of the Holy Spirit in the 1960's & '70's. John Wimber was the founder of the Vineyard Church movement.

When casting the vision for the Vineyard, John Wimber would say that the Vineyard vision is organic and it grows with the people of the Vineyard who are busy doing the stuff that Jesus did. I have always admired John Wimber's mold-breaking ability and his simplistic approach to changes that take place with any ministry that is successfully manifesting the ministry of Jesus and the works of His Kingdom upon the earth.

Though your core values will probably never change, (mine haven't), how you do what you do is sure to change. I think we should be prepared to let the vision be organic and grow with the team. The vision that God gives you is as dynamic as His word. You define what He shows you, you process it and begin to walk forward in it, and it develops as His living word develops on the inside of you and changes your life. He doesn't usually change His mind, but He is busy changing you and the world around you. A vision should produce change. We ought to be ready to let the vision organically change from season to season, from harvest to harvest.

From your core values and your purpose of ministry you now know why you want to construct this church/ministry/business. The vision that comes from the Holy Spirit will give you the ability to explain to the world what you do, and your mission statement will announce how you do it.

Remember that I said in the beginning that the question, "What is your vision?" should help you define what you do. And the question, "What is your mission?" should help you define how you do what you do.

The vision can, and perhaps should be lengthier than the core values and the purposes of this church/ministry. Here you can use descriptive words to make it plain and understandable to all who read the vision. The world needs to know what you do after they understand why you do what you do.

As we began this journey, we worked on what the Holy Spirit has said to you. It is from the notes you have made that we will begin to write the vision. From the documentation of the word of the Holy Spirit, we can mold and shape the vision of the church/ministry. That is how we can "make it plain upon tablets..."

A clear perspective of where you will be when you accomplish the works of the ministry is needed for writing both the vision and the mission. So, the vision starts with the target but includes what you do while getting there.

As you gather and build your team

around you, all will need to see where you are going and something similar to a roadmap can be drawn that will show the path. First, however, must be the kind of "site plan" for what it looks like when it is finished. When what you see is written you'll see that it has transformed into how you do the stuff of the ministry.

Having compiled all the information on the "word of the LORD," and having described all dreams, visions, and trances, all prophetic utterances, and desires of your heart, then explain how you feel. Ask yourself some fundamental questions about how you feel and your vision for ministry. Begin to write the description of: What does it look like when what the Holy Spirit said comes to pass?

Here are a couple of ideas:

- This is what it looks like when what we do is accomplished.

- This is what we do in the ministry and this is what happens when we do it.

Ask for God's help to translate what He is saying to you. If there are areas that are still vague, nebulous, or indefinite, ask the Holy Spirit to help you explain what He is saying to you, and to fill in any points that are vague. If there is anything that is wrong, let Him correct you. During this time with the Holy Spirit, be sensitive and receptive.

From the outcome of this encounter with the Spirit and the work that you have done in writing the vision down, your vision of your church/ministry can be procured and seen by others.

For example, I'll share with you the vision of Standsure Ministries and these steps from core values to ministry purpose and the why of what we do. From that point, we develop the ministry vision.

Standsure Ministries with Wayne C. & Irene Joy Anderson

Our Vision: (What we do.)

- ➢ We are traveling the world and manifesting the ministry of our Lord and Savior, Jesus Christ in the nations.

- ➢ We are releasing the Spirit of the Father that gives strength to many sons & daughters of the faith in various nations, being accessible to them and interacting with them.

- ➢ We are leading an apostolic family of Christ filled believers, multiplying disciples unto the nations of the world.

- ➢ We are using the revelatory gift that the Father has bestowed upon us to revive people's spirits and teach them the ways of the Kingdom of heaven.

- We help others found churches and houses of prayer to influence regions with the principles of the Kingdom of heaven.
- We are forming schools online courses and webinars to teach the multitudes the victorious messages of the Kingdom of heaven
- We are educating believers on how to wins souls and do great exploits for the name of Jesus Christ.
- We are leading the emerging Ecclesia into significant positions of authority as they manifest the Kingdom of heaven and the will of the Father upon the earth with measurable results.
- We are helping believers to experience revival in their churches, cities, regions, and nations.

5 Defining Your Mission

The phrase "mission statement" can sometimes be confusing to Christ believers and church leaders in that when we hear the word "missions" we automatically think of the ministry works that are being done overseas. However, a mission statement is not a statement about how we see or feel about ministries abroad, but a written declaration of how we accomplish our tasks, projects, and responsibilities. How do we run with the vision that we've seen? How do we do what we do?

I suppose we could think of the famous series Mission: Impossible and realize that the mission has no way of being accomplished. But there must be a way of accomplishment and just like the movie series how we do it is the exciting part.

Most of us who are excited about life have some kind of vision for the future. It makes us want to get up in the morning and it keeps us from the killer depression. As soon as there is vision our immediate response is how do I do what needs to be done for me to get from here to there? There are so many choices. That is what we describe in our mission statement. How literally do I reach what I see?

Although I'm directing you to outline how you will actually design how the ministry will work, (and the list could get long), some have also made their list into a concise statement that all can memorize and quote as an explanation of how you are going to accomplish your vision. If you'd like to do this you might check out some "mission statements" of other ministries or corporations for wording, ideas, or even catch their zeal in their mission statements. However, I believe that you will be more successful if you tell the world why. I believe that people want to feel your why and make it their why. Of course, there is a segment of the population that is looking for your how to see if they might be able to fill a position in getting meaningful things done.

I have found that the best way to do this is to sit down and reread your vision list of what you do. Take each thing you do and start explaining how you will do that. Let me give you an example just off the top of my head here.

Let's say, in your vision you have the statement that you are going to win the lost to Christ. In your missions list you need to describe how you are going to do that. Crusades? Door to door evangelism? House parties and bible studies? Street preaching? School assemblies? Special church services?

So, in this example, you might first make a similar list and then try to explain each effort on your list. Let's just do the last one: Special church services.

Example:
- We will have a special weekly

service every Saturday night that is specifically for winning the lost.

- To do so we will train people to reach out to those around them with calculated acts of love.

- We will collect the names of those people that need to be saved and we'll have a prayer meeting for each of the people whose name is on our list.

- We'll record our prayers for each person and replay the recorded prayer in the church 24 hours a day.

- We will begin to let people know that they are being prayed for and invite them to the special Saturday service that is structured with a salvation message and an opportunity to commit to Christ.

- We will continually develop our follow-up plans so that we can begin to disciple the new believers.

So, I'm just throwing these thoughts out so that I can then go back and fine tune them into something that is attainable and doable. I would want to articulate it better so that fellow believers can join in and run with it.

In hope of further helping you to understand what I'm saying about the mission statement (how you do what you do), I will present the mission statement of Standsure Ministries.

Standsure Ministries with Wayne C. & Irene Joy Anderson

Our Mission: (How we do what we do.)

- ➢ We prayerfully establish an itinerary of travel to many regions and nations making the name of Jesus famous throughout the world!

- We assemble believers into convenings, gatherings, dialog sessions, conference calls and conferences to educate them in the dynamics of the Kingdom of heaven.

- We prayerfully example the Father's love to a generation of fatherless, equipping them for the work of the ministry by instructions using all forms of media.

- We are teaching believers how to strengthen the family in every available media.

- We develop and maintain our websites with articles for revelatory learning.

- We present webinars conference calls on pertinent subjects for revelatory learning.

- We develop and maintain online

courses to better instruct and educate believers.

- We are training the emerging Ecclesia to take their authoritative position in the courts of heaven and change the world by the decrees and intercession.

- We publish books, articles and recorded video and audio messages with revelatory messages for believers to learn, understand and apply the dynamics of the Kingdom of heaven.

6 Let's Write The Charge

Our Charge, for the sake of Christ our King, will contain our banners.

If you have worked through each of the prior stages of writing the vision, then it's time to take a look at what you have done as a whole. Can you sense that there is a cultural development in what you have written? Will you be able to draw a team of people together to rally around the vision that you are now able to present them?

With the completed written vision, can

you start to see what a people group of this vision will look like in full array? Are they a force to be reckoned with? And, how would this force seem to those who are watching?

Further thoughts: Where will corporate body end up? What stands will be taken by all involved?

It is especially important to know what stand will be taken, by all those concerned with the project. The character and integrity of the ministry is formed by the charge made from the very beginning. For example, if honesty is expected, and intended, to be seen as a trait of the person or the entire group, then it should be written and read by all so that there are no questions as to how to respond to any given situation.

Every ministry is a covenant entity before God. It has, and develops; its own character and personality. What that character and personality will look like to the world, to other churches and ministers, and to the people who attend, will much depend upon what the leadership has become. Just as a person grows, matures, and develops in character and personality, so does the church/ministry.

Each person makes a contribution to the disposition of the group as a whole. Thus, each church/ministry makes a contribution to the character of the Body of Christ as a whole.

The word of God shows us that our heavenly Father has written out for us the identity of the body of Christ so that we can see where we are going and what we want to look like to everyone around us along the way. We know how to act and react, with whom to associate, where our treasure is to be found, and what we'll look like when He's finished with us.

The more we describe what we'll look

like as we complete the work that the Father of lights has given to us to do, the more equipped we will be to accomplish the task.

Relevant Strategies for the Church/Ministry:

What programs will be necessary to fulfill this vision?

What is the picture of the ministry? Can you graph it? Can you outline it? Can you box chart it? Can you draw a portrait of it? Most people can better understand and communicate with a graph, a drawing, or some sort of an outline that will become like a roadmap for the ministry.

The Father has appointed you to be an answer to needs and His Kingdom strategies. Therefore, you can begin to plan the ways that you will actualize the good works of God. Jesus Christ is always the answer. His Kingdom will never fail. The question that remains is, "How will you apply the works of His Kingdom?" Describe with detailed facts, not effectual feelings, the projects that the church/ministry will perform. This is similar to an ongoing "To-Do" list for the church/ministry.

What ministry outreaches will be necessary to fulfill this vision?

There must always be plans set forth to go out of our own gathering and reach toward others. We must cause the Kingdom of God to grow. This does not necessarily mean that we will always have to make our own church/ministry grow by the very instruments that we use. For example, we may feed the poor in an area of our city without even one of the poor that we are feeding, ever becoming active in our ministry, yet, we will experience growth because people want to help feed the poor.

What departments will be necessary to fulfill this vision?

How many others will it take to see the vision moving toward its goal? What people groups will have to be organized into a working force that will make things happen? In answering these questions, divisions can be made for organization and efficiency. Prayer can be directed to fill the needs as this makes known what those needs are.

Build a team to "do the work of the ministry."

Teamwork is the most potent kind of ministry. Working together in unity to accomplish His work has higher potential than does the workings of only a few. In this, the old proverbial statement is found to be true: "Why do the work of ten men, when you can get ten men to do the work?" People, systematically organized into people groups, doing ministry works that join one another at some point, will bring about joy and an unfathomable potential. Although Jesus was the firstborn from the dead and the only begotten son of the Father, all that He taught was "Team Ministry!" The team of 5-fold ministries' purpose is made clear in Ephesians 4:12: "for the equipping of the saints for the work of ministry, for the edifying of the body of Christ." (NKJV)

Let's Build a Ministry Plan.

Now we can begin the ministry plan. In the ministry plan, we will accomplish the "hands-on" work of the ministry. This is where the proverbial "rubber meets the road," that is, "How do we get things done?" There is an old business proverb that says, "If you fail to plan, you plan to fail."

You are never without a message; however, a basis of your messages is needed to show others just what you do. Then we must build a strategy for reaching the people that you want to reach.

What does the calendar look like for a year, for the seasons of the year, as well as the days and months? Then, where do you want to be in the next five years or so?

If you are an itinerate minister rather

than a church, you can now plan a campaign for your itinerating, as well as work in each church where you go to minister. You also need to have a plan for getting those preaching engagements.

Here are some examples of our charge as an itinerate ministry that may or may not help.

Standsure Ministries with Wayne C. & Irene Joy Anderson:

Relevant Strategies:

> We are traveling and preaching in church services, conferences and conventions to minister the presence of God and the anointing, revealing the glory of God in every worship service so that people will see Jesus and be changed.

- We are giving vision, direction and hope to people, churches, houses of prayer, intercessors and fellow ministries.
- We will continue to establish communication tools that will enable us to communicate with individuals, leaders and the multitudes.
- We endeavor to reveal strategies of supplying the needs to accomplish the work of ministry. This supply may include planning and organization, confidence, training, vision, equipment, the place of ministry, and setting individuals into the offices of ministry, etc.
- We are teaching the principles of successful living and a penetrating ministry life.
- Our book writing is for three arenas: 1) equipping believers

2) restoring faith in the miracles of Jesus Christ, and 3) teaching from our life messages.

➢ We are building relative audio and video messages with immediate online downloads (also CD/DVD) for tools of equipping and for believers to have revelatory understanding of the Kingdom of heaven.

➢ We operate a website that is a meeting place for many for partners, giving information, revelation, and organization.

➢ We are continually developing our financial partners giving them priority in our messages and communication. Our partners receive monthly news, articles, recorded messages, their own unique website loaded with revelatory teaching in all formats.

➢ We lead an apostolic family of believers that have impact and influence in the nations.

The Principles, which we have soundly ministered:

➢ The anointing and the manifest presence of God, the Father's overwhelming love for His believing children
➢ The substance of divine healing, by the laying on of hands, the prayer of faith and the Table of the Lord
➢ The fullness of the family life through the strengthening of relationships in marriages and parenting children, by example, by revelatory teaching, and by faith
➢ Established and ever increasing, deep-seated belief, for miracles, signs, and wonders to be

manifested – by example, prayer, and fasting

➢ Revealing the poor & needy, widows, orphans & aliens, as a benefit to the Church. By giving, strategizing, and making way for others to give, we will receive this great gain.

➢ Prosperity – by teaching, giving, and example.

Our Responsibilities:

➢ As a father of the faith and an example of God the Father, we must:

➢ Guide them, giving guidelines, and boundaries, to correct their course and train them up for their destiny

➢ Guide them into a deeper walk of faith and trust in Jesus Christ

➢ Give them Godly wisdom and

rescue

- ➢ Give them direction
- ➢ Give them inheritance
- ➢ Give them tools
- ➢ Give them hope
- ➢ Be an example of the anointing, and the presence of God, so that people will see and experience Jesus, knowing that when they see Jesus, they will be changed forever!
- ➢ Bring them Healing which is bread for the children and is found at His Table.

7 Consulting Apostles & Prophets

I sincerely believe that input from one or more qualified apostles or prophets will help you in your endeavors. To confer with an apostle and/or prophet, letting them deliberate over the vision and its effect upon the land, the city, the nation, and the Ecclesia of Jesus Christ will add Kingdom substance to the vision and the ministry. We can never stand alone. Every person in the body of Christ must be submitted to others, including the leaders and the leaders of leaders.

"Now ye are the body of Christ and members in particular. And God hath set some in the church, first apostles, secondarily prophets, thirdly teachers, after that miracles, then gifts of healing, helps, governments, diversities of tongues. Are all apostles? Are all prophets? Are all teachers? Are all workers of miracles?"

1 Corinthians 12: 27 - 29 KJV

Notice in these scriptures that we are all members in particular and have a specific part to play in the Body of Christ. We must let the apostles and prophets do their job, to see the body move forth.

"Believe in the LORD your God, so shall ye be established; believe his prophets, so shall ye prosper."

2 Chronicles 20:20 KJV

"Surely the Lord GOD will do nothing,

but he reveals his secret unto his servants the prophets."

Amos 3:7 KJV

Ephesians 2:20 shows us that the foundational ministries of the building, that God calls His Ecclesia, which is a spiritual tabernacle for He Himself to reside. This Ecclesia is founded upon the ministries of apostles & prophets. If a ministry, built upon the pretense that it will be moving by the Holy Spirit, is to begin in the biblical pattern and blueprint, it will be submitted to holy apostles & prophets. This submission should always be done carefully and prayerfully. Submission is not meant as control or slavery and bondage.

Let Others Read the Vision!

"Make it plain upon tablets, that he may run that reads it." –

Habakkuk

It is your responsibility to communicate the vision so that they can understand it. It is not right and proper for leadership to expect others to simply "catch" the vision. God has entrusted something extraordinary into your hands, and He expects you to handle it with care: That is The Vision. Take the responsibility of communicating the Vision in such a way that others, both corporately and individually, will understand and be able to run with it.

You must protect the vision so that the ministry does not run away from the intended purposes. Many will come and try to redirect the ministry away from the God-given vision.

Many ministries fail because someone is allowed to come in with another agenda and begins to lead the ministry and the people away from the original vision. When the vision is made clear, this becomes very hard to do without being noticed. Protect the vision. Let qualified apostles and prophets help you protect the vision.

Casting nets and proclaiming the vision.

In his book "10 Simple Secrets of the World's Greatest Business Communicators,"[4] Carmine Gallo gives the business history of some historically successful business people and corporate managers. Gallo reveals an essential fact

---

[4] 10 Simple Secrets of the World's Greatest Business Communicators, by Carmine Gallo; Copyright © 2006 by Carmine Gallo; Publisher Sourcebooks, Inc.;sourcebooks.com; available on Amazon in book and ebook.

about the success of a corporation to be its leadership's ability to cast the vision of the company.

How you cast the vision means the difference between mediocre ministry accomplishments and causing a movement to take place. It is wrong to believe in the disheartening idea of "build it, and they'll come." This is proven to be totally wrong by millions of ministry "survivors." No matter how well you preach and sing, etc., there is no substitute for a well written and established vision and a leader that can skillfully cast the vision.

Sadly, I know very few people in ministry that sincerely study and learn from others the art of casting their vision. And the one who can both learn and then teach others to cast the vision is the one who has continual breakthroughs and is bound to affect the world.

Please give this some serious thought and start asking questions and getting the answers that are foundationally needed.

A growing library of books by Standsure Press:

40 Days of Prayer & Healing
By Wayne C. & Irene Joy Anderson
standsure.net/40days

Change The World with Prayer
By Wayne C. Anderson
standsure.net/changetheworld

Home Is Where The Throne Is
By Wayne C. Anderson
Available in paperback & Kindle, etc.
standsure.net/throneroom

Communing With The Father at
the Table Of The Lord
By Wayne C. Anderson
standsure.net/communion

Write the Vision
Outlining & organizing your ministry
By Wayne C. Anderson
standsure.net/writethevision

Wayne C. Anderson
is equipping the saints of the emerging
Kingdom through his 3 Life Messages:

1. The Substance of Heaven

2. The Table of the Lord

3. Ecclesia Prayer & Intercession

Audio & Video is available in a growing number of subjects from the power of these 3 Life Messages that the Holy Spirit has given to Wayne to proclaim.

These messages are available in a number of medias at:

Standsure.net/shop

Partner with Wayne C. & Irene Joy Anderson

- ✓ Benefits of financial partnering:
- ✓ Monthly messages in CD & mp3 formats
- ✓ Newsletter Monthly Article
- ✓ Partners' Website: partnersof.standsure.net
- ✓ Audio mp3 downloads
- ✓ Table Of The Lord Videos
- ✓ Product Discount Coupons
- ✓ Partner's Podcasts

Standsure.net/partner

Our Partner's Website has a plethora of learning tools that are free to our financial supporters.

You can find many of Wayne C. Anderson's books at Amazon.com

Please check out our Amazon author page:

Amazon.com/author/waynecanderson

You can learn more about the ministries of Wayne C. Anderson online:

Standsure Ministries with

Wayne C. & Irene Joy Anderson

Standsure.net

Empowering Online Courses

with Wayne C. Anderson

learning.iamtheway.org

Our apostolic network:

International Apostolic Ministries

iamtheway.org

ABOUT THE AUTHOR

Wayne C Anderson and his wife Irene Joy Anderson live in Meridian, Idaho, the western foothills of the Rocky Mountains. Wayne & Irene met and married in Seattle, Washington, and after near 45 years of marriage, are the delighted parents of 7 children, 15 grandchildren.

While in Seattle, Wayne spent over 12 years as a firefighter for the City of Seattle, and for more than 20 years Wayne & Irene pastored in South Seattle. Wayne was the 7th president of the Ministerial Fellowship of the USA, originally founded by John G. Lake. Much of Wayne's ministry has been that of an influential national and international leader. He was one of the principle leaders of Seattle Revival Center, which birthed a revival in the mid 1990's, having also been at the epicenter of revivals in Finland, Mexico, Africa and the US.

Wayne has now established churches and ministries in numerous countries and is the founding Presiding Apostolic Director of International Apostolic Ministries, a fast growing apostolic network.

Wayne & his son Joshua were honorably summoned to appear before the current Sanhedrin in Jerusalem on June 4th, 2013, which was a momentous and life changing experience.

Wayne periodically speaks with governmental leaders in the United States and other nations with an anointed voice of wisdom, which changes the hearts of leaders. He is an in-depth Bible teacher with growing revelatory development toward fathering and miracles and the expansion of our worldview, while he continues to travel the world preaching & equipping believers with keys of the kingdom of God. As an author and speaker, Wayne is diligently working to change the landscape of the Kingdom worldview of believers around the globe.

Standsure Ministries
With Wayne C. & Irene Joy Anderson
3313 W Cherry LN #656
Meridian ID 83642 USA
standsureministries@standsure.net

Made in the
USA
Middletown, DE